CAJUN COOKING

GALLERY BOOKS
An Imprint of W. H. Smith Publishers Inc.
112 Madison Avenue
New York City 10016

INTRODUCTION

Driven from their lands in Canada by the British in the late 18th century, the people from the French colony of Acadia moved south to settle in the fertile bayou country of southern Louisiana. They made a home for themselves in the swampy, mysterious marshland around New Orleans, and a colorful Cajun culture, part French and part American, evolved.

The food was based on French country cooking, but adapted to the local ingredients. Cajun cooks exchanged ideas with Creole cooks, and some of the Spanish, West Indian and African influence of the latter crept into the Cajun repertoire.

Both Cajun and Creole cooking rely on seafood, rice, herbs, peppers and green onions as staple ingredients, and both are frequently spicy and hot in character. Whatever the similarities or differences, one thing is certain, Cajun food is among the most spirited in America today.

SERVES 6

SHRIMP BISQUE

This classic Cajun recipe makes a first
course or a full meal. It isn't a smooth
purée like its French counterpart.

3 tbsps butter or margarine
1 onion, finely chopped
1 red pepper, seeded and finely chopped
2 sticks celery, finely chopped
1 clove garlic, minced
Pinch dry mustard and cayenne pepper
2 tsps paprika
3 tbsps flour
4 cups fish stock
1 sprig thyme and bay leaf
8oz raw, peeled shrimp
Salt and pepper
Snipped chives

Step 2 Cook the mustard, cayenne, paprika and flour briefly until the mixture darkens in color.

1. Melt the butter or margarine and add the onion, pepper, celery and garlic. Cook gently to soften.

2. Stir in the mustard, cayenne, paprika and flour. Cook about 3 minutes over gentle heat, stirring occasionally.

3. Pour on the stock gradually, stirring until well blended. Add the thyme and bay leaf and bring to the boil. Reduce the heat and simmer about 5 minutes or until thickened, stirring occasionally.

4. Add the shrimp and cook until pink and curled, about 5 minutes. Season with salt and pepper to taste and top with snipped chives before serving.

Step 3 Pour on the stock gradually and stir or whisk until well blended.

Step 4 Use kitchen scissors to snip the chives finely over the top of the soup before serving.

Cook's Notes

Time
Preparation takes about 20 minutes and cooking takes about 8-10 minutes.

Variation
If using peeled, cooked shrimp add just before serving and heat through for about 2 minutes only.

Cook's Tip
Cook spices such as paprika briefly before adding any liquid to develop their flavor and eliminate harsh taste.

SERVES 4-6

HOT PEPPER EGG SALAD

Cajun cooks excel at using what is to hand, and this salad is
made with just those kinds of ingredients.

4 eggs
Half a bunch of green onions, chopped
Half a small red pepper, chopped
Half a small green pepper, chopped
4oz cooked, peeled shrimp
1 small jar artichoke hearts, drained and quartered

Dressing

6 tbsps oil
2 tbsps white wine vinegar
1 clove garlic, finely chopped
1 tsp dry mustard
1-2 tsps hot red pepper flakes, or 1 small fresh chili,
    seeded and finely chopped
Salt

1. Prick the large end of the eggs with an egg pricker or a needle.

2. Lower each egg carefully into boiling, salted water. Bring the water back to the boil, rolling the eggs in the water with the bowl of a spoon.

3. Cook the eggs for 9 minutes once the water comes back to the boil. Drain and rinse under cold water until completely cool. Peel and quarter. Combine the eggs with the other ingredients in a large bowl.

4. Mix the dressing ingredients together using a whisk to get a thick emulsion.

5. Pour the dressing over the salad and mix carefully so that the eggs do not break up.

6. Serve on beds of shredded lettuce, if desired.

Step 2 Lower each egg carefully into the water and roll around with the bowl of a spoon to set the yolk.

Step 4 Mix the dressing ingredients together using a whisk to get a thick emulsion.

Cook's Notes

 Time
Preparation takes about 25 minutes and cooking takes about 9 minutes to boil the eggs.

 **Preparation**
If preparing the eggs in advance, leave in the shells and in cold water. This will prevent a gray ring forming around the yolks.

 Cook's Tip
Rolling the eggs around in the hot water helps to set the yolk in the center of the white and makes sliced or quartered eggs more attractive.

SERVES 6

GUMBO Z'HERBES

Gumbo is an African word for okra, which
helps to thicken this soup-stew. Z'Herbes
refers to all the greens that go into it.

1lb spring greens, collard, mustard, beet or turnip greens
8oz spinach, well washed
4oz chicory (Belgian endive)
8oz green cabbage leaves
1 large bunch watercress, well washed
1 large bunch parsley, well washed
6 carrot and radish tops (if available)
4 cups water
Salt, pepper and a pinch cayenne
2 tbsps butter or margarine
1 large red pepper, seeded and coarsely chopped
Half a bunch green onions, coarsely chopped
8oz okra, trimmed and sliced
1 bay leaf
1 tsp thyme
Pinch cinnamon and nutmeg

Step 1 Using a small, sharp knife, trim down any coarse stalks from the greens, spinach or cabbage.

Step 3 Purée the vegetables in a food processor or a food mill until very smooth.

1. Trim any coarse stalks on the cabbage and spinach and wash both well. Wash greens, chicory, watercress, parsley and carrot and radish tops.

2. Bring water to the boil in a large stock pot and add the greens, spinach, cabbage, chicory, watercress, parsley and carrot and radish tops. Return the mixture to the boil, reduce the heat and simmer, partially covered, for about 2 hours.

3. Strain and reserve the liquid. Purée the vegetables in a food processor until smooth, and return to the rinsed out pot. Measure the liquid and make up to 3 cups with water, if necessary.

4. Melt the butter or margarine, cook the peppers, onions and okra briefly and add to the gumbo. Add the bay leaf, thyme and spices and cook a further 30 minutes over gentle heat. Remove the bay leaf, adjust the seasoning and serve.

Cook's Notes

Time
Preparation takes about 25 minutes and cooking takes 2 hours and 30 minutes.

Preparation
Fresh spinach is often very sandy, so wash at least 3 times before cooking, changing the water every time.

Cook's Tip
Okra will help to thicken the soup. If the soup is still too thin, add 1 tbsp cornstarch dissolved in 2 tbsps cold water. Bring to the boil, stirring until the cornstarch thickens and clears.

CRAB MEAT BALLS

Delicious as a first course or a cocktail
snack, crab meat balls can be made ahead,
then coated and fried at the last minute.

1lb fresh or frozen crab meat, chopped finely
4 slices white bread, crusts removed and made into
    crumbs
1 tbsp butter or margarine
1 tbsp flour
½ cup milk
½ red or green chili, seeded and finely chopped
1 green onion, finely chopped
1 tbsp chopped parsley
Salt
Flour
2 eggs, beaten
Dry breadcrumbs
Oil for frying

1. Combine the crab meat with the fresh breadcrumbs and set aside.

2. Melt the butter and add the flour off the heat. Stir in the milk and return to moderate heat. Bring to the boil, stirring constantly.

3. Stir the white sauce into the crab meat and bread-crumbs, adding the chili, onion and parsley. Season with salt to taste, cover and allow to cool completely.

4. Shape the cold mixture into 1 inch balls with floured hands.

5. Coat with beaten egg using a fork to turn balls in the mixture or use a pastry brush to coat with egg.

Step 4 Flour hands well and shape cold crab mixture into balls.

Step 5 Brush on beaten egg or dip into egg to coat.

6. Coat with the dry breadcrumbs.

7. Fry in oil in a deep sauté pan, saucepan or deep-fat fryer at 350°F until golden brown and crisp, about 3 minutes per batch of 6. Turn occasionally while frying.

8. Drain on paper towels and sprinkle lightly with salt.

Cook's Notes

Time
Preparation takes about 40-50 minutes, including time for the mixture to cool. A batch of 6 balls takes about 3 minutes to cook.

Variation
Use finely chopped shrimp instead of crab meat. Omit chili if desired, or use a quarter red or green pepper.

Economy
Cooked whitefish such as haddock or whiting can be substituted for half of the crab meat. Crab sticks can also be used.

SERVES 8-10

RED BEAN AND RED PEPPER SOUP

Red beans are very popular in southern Louisiana, and here
they make a hearty soup combined with red peppers and red wine.

1lb dried red kidney beans
Water to cover
2 onions, coarsely chopped
3 sticks celery, coarsely chopped
2 bay leaves
Salt and pepper
3 large red peppers, seeded and finely chopped
4 tbsps red wine
10 cups chicken stock
Lemon wedges and 4 chopped hard-boiled eggs to
    garnish

3. Bring to the boil over high heat, stirring occasionally.
Reduce the heat and allow to simmer, partially covered, for
about 3 hours, or until the beans are completely tender.

4. Remove the bay leaves and purée the soup in a food
processor or blender.

5. Serve garnished with the chopped hard-boiled egg.
Serve lemon wedges on the side.

Step 2 Combine
the beans with
the other
ingredients in a
large stock pot
and pour on
enough chicken
stock to cover.

Step 1 Soak the
beans overnight in
enough water to
cover, or boil for
two minutes and
leave to soak for
an hour. The
beans will swell in
size.

Step 3 When the
beans are soft
enough to mash
easily, remove bay
leaves and purée
the soup.

1. Soak the beans in the water overnight. Alternatively,
bring them to the boil and boil rapidly for 2 minutes. Leave
to stand for 1 hour.

2. Drain off the liquid and add the onions, celery, bay
leaves, salt and pepper, red peppers, red wine and stock.

Cook's Notes

Time
Preparation takes about 25
minutes, with overnight
soaking for the beans. Cooking takes
about 3 hours.

Watchpoint
It is dangerous to eat dried
pulses that are not thoroughly
cooked. Make sure the beans are very
soft before puréeing.

Freezing
The soup may be prepared
and puréed in advance and
frozen for up to 3 months. Freeze in
small containers so that the soup will
defrost faster. Defrost at room
temperature, breaking the mixture up
with a fork as the soup defrosts.

SERVES 6

GREEN RICE

Fresh herbs are a must for this rice dish, but use whatever mixture suits your taste or complements the main course.

2 tbsps oil
2 tbsps butter
¾ cup uncooked long-grain rice
2 cups boiling water
Pinch salt and pepper
3oz mixed chopped fresh herbs (parsley, thyme, marjoram, basil)
1 small bunch green onions, finely chopped

Step 3 Cook very gently for about 20 minutes, or until all the liquid has been absorbed by the rice and the grains are tender.

Step 1 Cook the rice in the oil and butter until it begins to turn opaque.

Step 4 Stir the onions and herbs into the rice and fluff up the grains with a fork.

1. Heat the oil in a large, heavy-based saucepan and add the butter. When foaming, add the rice and cook over moderate heat for about 2 minutes, stirring constantly.

2. When the rice begins to look opaque, add the water, salt and pepper and bring to the boil, stirring occasionally.

3. Cover the pan and reduce the heat. Simmer very gently,

without stirring, for about 20 minutes or until all the liquid has been absorbed and the rice is tender.

4. Chop the herbs very finely and stir into the rice along with the chopped green onions. Cover the pan and leave to stand for about 5 minutes before serving.

Cook's Notes

Time
Preparation takes about 20 minutes and cooking takes about 20-25 minutes.

Serving Ideas
Serve as a side dish to any meat, poultry or game recipe.

Cook's Tip
The rice must simmer very slowly if it is to absorb all the water without overcooking. Add extra water or pour some off as necessary during cooking, depending on how much liquid the rice has absorbed.

SERVES 6

MAQUE CHOUX

Sweetcorn is essential to this recipe, but
other vegetables can be added, too. In true
Cajun style, use what you have to hand.

4 tbsps oil
2 tbsps butter or margarine
2 medium-size onions, peeled and finely chopped
1 clove garlic, crushed
1 medium-size green pepper, seeded and cut into small
 dice
6 tomatoes, peeled, seeded and diced
8oz fresh corn kernels or frozen corn
1 cup chicken or vegetable stock
Pinch salt
½ tsp cayenne pepper
4 tbsps heavy cream

Step 1 Cook the
onions and garlic
until soft and
transparent but
not browned.

1. Heat the oil in a large casserole and add the butter.
When foaming, add the onions and garlic and cook,
stirring frequently, for about 5 minutes or until both are soft
and transparent but not browned.

2. Add the green pepper, tomatoes, corn and stock. Bring
to the boil over high heat.

3. Reduce the heat, partially cover the casserole and allow
to cook slowly for about 10 minutes, or until the corn is
tender. Add the cayenne pepper and salt and stir in the
cream. Heat through and serve immediately.

Step 2 Add the
vegetables and
liquid to the
onions and cook
until the corn is
tender.

Step 3 Stir in the
cream and return
to the heat to
warm through.
Serve
immediately.

Cook's Notes

Time
Preparation takes about 25
minutes. Cooking takes about
10 minutes for frozen corn and slightly
longer for fresh corn.

Variation
Use canned tomatoes,
coarsely chopped. Make up
the tomato liquid to the required
measurement with water. If desired,
fresh chili peppers may be used in
place of the cayenne pepper. Use half
to one whole chili pepper according to
taste. Cream may be omitted, if
desired.

Cook's Tip
Sweetcorn toughens if cooked
at too high a temperature for
too long, or if boiled too rapidly.

SERVES 6

SWEET POTATO AND SAUSAGE CASSEROLE

This close relative of the French soufflé is easier to make, and includes two Southern favorites — sweet potatoes and sausage.

2lbs sweet potatoes
2 tbsps oil
8oz sausage meat
1 small onion, finely chopped
2 sticks celery, finely chopped
½ green pepper, finely chopped
Pinch sage and thyme
Pinch salt and pepper
2 eggs, separated

Step 3 Brown the sausage meat in oil, mashing with a fork to break up lumps as the meat cooks.

Step 4 Add the egg yolks to the potato mixture, beating well with a wooden spoon.

Step 4 Whisk the egg whites until stiff but not dry.

1. Peel the sweet potatoes and cut them into 2 inch pieces. Place in boiling water to cover and add a pinch of salt. Cook quickly, uncovered, for about 20 minutes or until the sweet potatoes are tender to the point of a knife. Drain them well and leave them to dry.

2. Purée the potatoes using a potato masher.

3. While the potatoes are cooking, heat the oil in a large frying pan and add the sausage meat. Cook briskly, breaking up with a fork until the meat is golden brown. Add the onion, celery and green pepper, and cook for a further 5 minutes. Add the sage, thyme and a pinch of seasoning.

4. Beat the egg yolks into the mashed sweet potatoes and, using an electric mixer or a hand whisk, beat the egg whites until stiff but not dry.

5. Drain any excess fat from the sausage meat and combine it with the sweet potatoes. Fold in the whisked egg whites until thoroughly incorporated. Spoon the mixture into a well-buttered casserole dish or soufflé dish and bake in a preheated 375°F oven until well risen and brown on the top, about 25-30 minutes. Serve immediately.

Cook's Notes

 Time
Preparation takes about 35 minutes and cooking takes a total of 45 minutes.

 Serving Ideas
Serve as a side dish with poultry, or on its own as a light main course.

 Cook's Tip
Since this mixture is heavier than a normal soufflé mixture, do not expect it to rise as high.

MAKES 8

CAJUN PIES

We've baked this traditional meat pie
in individual portions. It's spicy hot,
so add cayenne gradually to taste.

Pastry

3 tbsps butter or margarine
2 eggs
4-6 tbsps milk or water
2½-3½ cups all-purpose flour
Pinch sugar and salt

Filling

2 tbsps butter or margarine
½ small onion, finely chopped
½ small green pepper, finely chopped
1 stick celery, finely chopped
1 clove garlic, crushed
¾lb ground pork
1 bay leaf, finely crushed
1 tsp cayenne pepper
Pinch salt
2 tbsps flour
1 cup beef stock
1 tbsp tomato paste
1 tsp dried thyme

Step 7 Spread the filling on half of each pastry circle and brush the edges with water.

Step 8 Fold over and seal the edges together, pressing them firmly. Crimp with a fork.

1. To prepare the pastry, soften the butter or margarine in a food processor or with an electric mixer until creamy. Beat in the eggs one at a time and add the milk or water.

2. Sift in 2½ cups flour, sugar and salt and mix until blended. If necessary, add the remaining flour gradually until the mixture forms a ball. Wrap well and refrigerate about 30 minutes.

3. Melt the butter or margarine in a large frying pan and cook the onion, pepper, celery, garlic and pork over moderate heat. Break up the meat with a fork as it cooks.

4. Add the bay leaf, cayenne pepper, salt and flour and cook, scraping the bottom of the pan often, until the flour browns.

5. Pour on the stock and stir in the tomato paste and

thyme. Bring to the boil and cook, stirring occasionally, until thickened. Chill thoroughly and remove the bay leaf.

6. Divide the pastry into 8 pieces and roll each out to a circle about ⅛ inch thick.

7. Spread the chilled filling on half of each circle to within ½ inch of the edge. Brush the edge with water.

8. Fold over and seal the edges together firmly. Crimp the edges with a fork.

9. Heat oil in a deep sauté pan or a deep fat fryer to about 350°F. Fry 2 or 3 pies at a time for about 2 minutes, holding them under the surface of the oil with a metal spoon to brown evenly. Remove from the oil with a draining spoon and drain on paper towels. Serve immediately.

Cook's Notes

Time
Preparation takes about 30-40 minutes, and cooking takes about 15 minutes for the filling and 2 minutes for each batch of 2 pies.

Cook's Tip
The dough may be prepared in advance and kept in a refrigerator for about 2 days.

Variation
Ground beef may be substituted for the pork. Double the quantity of vegetables for a vegetarian filling.

SERVES 6

SEAFOOD GUMBO FILÉ

Either filé powder, made from sassafras leaves,
or okra gives a Cajun gumbo its characteristic
texture. Gumbos are good without filé, too.

1lb cooked, unpeeled shrimp
Half quantity spice mixture (see Shellfish Boil)
5 cups water
4 tbsps butter or margarine
1 onion, peeled and sliced
1 green pepper, seeded and sliced
2 cloves garlic, finely chopped
3 tbsps flour
½ tsp thyme
1 bay leaf
2 tbsps chopped parsley
Dash Worcester sauce
12 oysters, shelled
8oz tomatoes, peeled and chopped
2 tbsps filé powder (optional)
Salt and pepper
Cooked rice

Step 1 Peel the shrimp adding the heads, tail shell, legs and roe, if present, to the spice mixture in a large stock pot.

Step 3 Loosen the oysters from their shells and add to the hot gumbo. If desired, strain the oyster liquid through a very fine mesh strainer.

1. Peel the shrimp and reserve the shells. Mix shells with the spice mixture and water and bring to the boil in a large stock pot. Reduce the heat and allow to simmer for about 20 minutes.

2. Melt the butter or margarine and, when foaming, add the onion, green pepper, garlic and flour. Cook slowly, stirring constantly until the flour is a pale golden brown. Gradually strain on the stock, discarding the shells and spice mixture. Add the thyme and bay leaf and stir well. Bring to the boil and then simmer until thick.

3. Add the parsley and the Worcester sauce to taste. Add the oysters, peeled shrimp and tomatoes and heat through gently to cook the oysters.

4. Stir in the filé powder and leave to stand to thicken. Adjust the seasoning and serve over rice.

Cook's Notes

Time
Preparation takes about 25-30 minutes and cooking takes about 20-25 minutes.

Variation
If they are available, use raw, unpeeled shrimp and cook with the water and the spice mixture until they turn pink and curl up. Drain them, reserving the liquid. Peel and return the shells to the stock. Re-boil the stock and allow to simmer for about 15 minutes.

Cook's Tip
If filé powder is not available, use equal portions of butter or margarine and flour mixed together to a paste. Add a bit of the paste at a time to the gumbo, and boil in between additions until the desired thickness is reached.

SERVES 4-6

SHELLFISH BOIL

This is the Cajun way to cook seafood.
Drained seafood is piled onto newspaper-covered
tables for everyone to dig in.

3 quarts water
1 lemon, quartered
1 onion, cut in half but not peeled
1 celery stick, cut in 3 pieces
2 cloves garlic, left whole
Pinch salt
4 bay leaves, finely crumbled
4 dried red chili peppers, crumbled
1 tbsp each whole cloves, whole allspice, coriander seed
    and mustard seed
1 tbsp dill weed, fresh or dry
2 tsps celery seed
1lb raw, unpeeled shrimp
2lbs mussels, well scrubbed

Step 3 Remove the seaweed beards and any barnacles from the mussel shells.

Step 2 Add the shrimp to the boiling liquid and cook them until pink and curled.

1. Place the water, lemon, onion, celery, garlic, salt, bay leaves and spices together in a large pot and cover. Bring to the boil, reduce the heat and cook slowly for 20 minutes.

2. Add the shrimp in two batches and cook until pink and curled. Remove with a draining spoon.

3. Remove the seaweed beards from the mussels, and discard any that do not close when tapped.

4. Add mussels to the pot and cook, stirring frequently, for about 5 minutes or until shells have opened. Discard any that do not open.

5. Spoon shrimp and mussels into serving bowls and serve immediately.

Cook's Notes

Time
Preparation takes about 30 minutes, cooking takes about 20 minutes to boil the stock and about 5 minutes for each batch of shrimp and mussels.

Serving Ideas
Serve as an appetizer, or double the quantity for a main course.

Variation
Usually crawfish are cooked in this way. Crabs are also used.

SERVES 4

BLACKENED FISH

Cajun cooks all have their own special recipes for the spice mixture, but all agree that the food should have a *very* brown crust when properly blackened.

4 fish fillets, about 8oz each
1 cup unsalted butter
1 tbsp paprika
1 tsp garlic powder
1 tsp cayenne pepper
½ tsp ground white pepper
1 tsp finely ground black pepper
2 tsps salt
1 tsp dried thyme

1. Melt the butter and pour about half into each of four custard cups and set aside.

2. Brush each fish fillet liberally with the remaining butter on both sides.

3. Mix together the spices and thyme and sprinkle generously on each side of the fillets, patting it on by hand.

4. Heat a large frying pan and add about 1 tbsp butter per fish fillet. When the butter is hot, add the fish, skin side down first.

5. Turn the fish over when the underside is very brown and repeat with the remaining side. Add more butter as necessary during cooking.

6. When the top side of the fish is very dark brown, repeat with the remaining fish fillets, keeping them warm while cooking the rest.

7. Serve the fish immediately with the cups of butter for dipping.

Step 2 Use a pastry brush to coat the fish well on both sides with the melted butter. Alternatively, spoon the butter over or dip the fish in the butter.

Step 3 Mix the seasoning ingredients together well and press firmly onto both sides of the fish to coat.

Step 5 Cook the underside and topside of the fish until very dark brown.

Cook's Notes

Time
Preparation takes about 20 minutes and cooking takes about 2 minutes per side for each fillet.

Variation
Red fish or pompano is the usual choice. If these fish are not available, substitute other varieties of fish fillets or steaks that are approximately ¾ inch thick.

Preparation
The fish must be very dark brown on the top and the bottom before serving. Leave at least 2 minutes before attempting to turn the fish over.

SERVES 4

TROUT WITH OYSTER STUFFING

Oysters are used freely in Cajun cooking since they're plentiful in this part of the world. They make a luxurious stuffing for whole fish.

4 whole trout, about 8oz each
½ cup butter or margarine
1 onion, finely chopped
2 sticks celery, finely chopped
1 small red pepper, seeded and finely chopped
4 green onions, finely chopped
1 clove garlic, crushed
12 oysters on the half shell
2 tsps chopped parsley
1 tsp chopped fresh dill
¼ tsp white pepper
¼ tsp cayenne pepper
¼ tsp black pepper
Pinch salt
1 cup dry breadcrumbs
2 small eggs, lightly beaten

1. Wash the trout well inside and pat dry.

2. Melt half the butter or margarine in a medium saucepan. Add onions, celery, red pepper, green onions and garlic. Cook over a moderate heat for about 3 minutes to soften the vegetables.

3. Remove the oysters from the shells with a sharp knife and add them to the vegetables. Strain and reserve any oyster liquid. Cook the oysters about 2 minutes, breaking them up into large pieces while they cook. Stir in the white pepper, cayenne pepper and black pepper, dill and parsley.

4. Remove from the heat, add the breadcrumbs and gradually beat in the egg, adding just enough to hold the

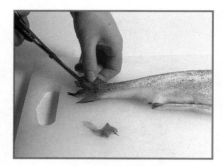

Step 1 Trim the fins, neaten the tail of the trout and rinse well. Pat dry.

Step 5 Spoon some of the stuffing into the cavity of each fish.

stuffing ingredients together. Season with salt.

5. Stuff the cavity of each trout with an equal amount of the stuffing and place the trout in a baking dish.

6. Spoon over the remaining butter and bake, uncovered, in a pre-heated 350°F oven for about 25 minutes. Brown under a pre-heated broiler before serving, if desired.

Cook's Notes

Time
Preparation takes about 30 minutes and cooking takes about 30 minutes.

Variation
Other varieties of fish, such as sea bass, gray mullet or red snapper, can also be used.

Economy
Since oysters are expensive, they may be omitted from the recipe or may be replaced with mussels, if desired. Canned oysters, which are somewhat cheaper, may also be used.

SERVES 2

BARBECUED SHRIMP

It's the sauce rather than the cooking method that
gives this dish its name. It's spicy, zippy and *hot*.

1lb large shrimp, cooked and unpeeled
½ cup unsalted butter
1 tsp each white, black and cayenne pepper
Pinch salt
1 tsp each chopped fresh thyme, rosemary and
   marjoram
1 clove garlic, crushed
1 tsp Worcester sauce
½ cup fish stock
4 tbsps dry white wine
Cooked rice

Remove the shrimp and set them aside.

3. Add the Worcester sauce, stock and wine to the
ingredients in the pan. Bring to the boil and cook for about
3 minutes to reduce. Add salt to taste.

4. Arrange the shrimp on a bed of rice and pour over the
sauce to serve.

Step 1 Remove
the legs and eyes
from the shrimp.
Leave on the long
antennae, if
desired.

Step 2 Melt the
butter and add
the spices and
herbs and
shrimp, and cook
briefly.

Step 3 Add the
Worcester sauce,
wine and stock to
the pan and boil
rapidly to reduce.

1. Remove the eyes and the legs from the shrimp.

2. Melt the butter in a large frying pan and add the white
pepper, black pepper, cayenne pepper, herbs and garlic.
Add the shrimp and toss over heat for a few minutes.

Cook's Notes

Time
Preparation takes about 15
minutes and cooking takes
about 5 minutes.

Preparation
Because the shrimp are pre-
cooked, cook them very
briefly again, just to heat through. Use
uncooked, unpeeled shrimp if
possible. Cook these until they curl and
turn pink.

Serving Ideas
Serve with the recipe for
Green Rice or use plain boiled
rice. The shrimp may also be served
cold. If serving cold, prepare the sauce
with 6 tbsps oil instead of the butter.

SERVES 4

CRAWFISH PIE

This seafood, plentiful in southern Louisiana, is
used in many delicious ways. The boiling mixture adds
spice, and the browned flour a nutty taste and good color.

Pastry
2 cups all-purpose flour, sifted
Pinch salt
½-¾ cup butter or margarine
Cold water

1lb raw crawfish or shrimp
½ quantity spice mixture for Shellfish Boil (see recipe)

Filling
3 tbsps oil
3 tbsps flour
½ green pepper, seeded and finely diced
2 green onions, finely chopped
1 stick celery, finely chopped
1 cup light cream
Salt and pepper

Step 6 Roll the pastry out thinly and use a rolling pin to transfer it to the baking dish.

1. Sift the flour into a bowl with a pinch of salt and rub in the butter or margarine until the mixture resembles fine breadcrumbs. Add enough cold water to bring the mixture together. Knead into a ball, wrap well and chill for about 30 minutes before use.

2. Combine the spice mixture with about 2½ cups water. Bring to the boil and add the crawfish or shrimp. Cook for about 5 minutes, stirring occasionally until the shellfish curl up. Remove from the liquid and leave to drain.

3. Heat the oil in a small saucepan for the filling and add the flour. Cook slowly, stirring constantly until the flour turns a rich dark brown.

4. Add the remaining filling ingredients, stirring constantly while adding the cream. Bring to the boil, reduce the heat and cook for about 5 minutes. Add the crawfish or shrimp to the sauce.

5. Divide the pastry into 4 and roll out each portion on a lightly-floured surface to about ¼ inch thick.

6. Line individual flan or pie dishes with the pastry, pushing it carefully onto the base and down the sides, taking care not to stretch it. Trim off excess pastry and reserve.

7. Place a sheet of wax paper or foil on the pastry and pour on rice, pasta or baking beans to come halfway up the sides. Bake the pastry blind for about 10 minutes in a preheated 400°F oven.

8. Remove the paper and beans and bake for an additional 5 minutes to cook the base.

9. Spoon in the filling and roll out any trimmings to make a lattice pattern on top. Bake a further 10 minutes to brown the lattice and heat the filling. Cool slightly before serving.

Cook's Notes

 Time
Preparation takes about 30 minutes and cooking takes about 10 minutes for the filling and 25 minutes to finish the dish.

 Cook's Tip
Baking the pastry blind helps it to crisp on the base and brown evenly without overcooking the filling.

Serving Ideas
Serve as a light main course with a salad, or make smaller pies to serve as a first course.

SERVES 4

CRAWFISH ÉTOUFÉE

This is a thick stew usually made with the local seafood.

⅓ cup butter or margarine
1 small onion, chopped
1lb crawfish or shrimp
6 tbsps flour
1 cup water or fish stock
1 tbsp tomato paste
2 tbsps chopped parsley
2 tsps chopped dill
Salt and pepper
2 tsps tabasco or to taste
Cooked rice

Step 1 Cook the onion and crawfish or shrimp quickly until it curls up.

1. Melt half the butter or margarine, add the onion and cook to soften slightly. Add scampi and cook quickly until it curls. Remove to a plate.

2. Add the flour to the pan and cook slowly until golden brown, stirring frequently.

3. Pour on the water and stir vigorously to blend. Add tomato paste and bring to the boil. Add parsley, dill, tabasco and seasoning to taste and return the onions and the scampi to the sauce. Heat through for 5 minutes and serve over rice.

Step 3 Add the water gradually, stirring vigorously. The mixture should be very thick.

Step 3 Return the crawfish or shrimp and onions to the sauce to heat through. Juices from both will thin down the sauce.

Cook's Notes

Time
Preparation takes about 20 minutes and cooking takes about 15 minutes.

Watchpoint
Shrimp, scampi and other types of seafood become very tough if cooked too quickly or over heat that is too high.

Preparation
The sauce must be very thick, so add the water gradually, reserving some to add once the sauce comes to the boil.

SERVES 4

SEAFOOD PAN ROAST

This mixture of oysters and crab is a descendant
of French gratin recipes. It's quick to make,
and other seafood may be added.

24 small oysters on the half shell
1 cup fish stock
1 cup light cream
⅓ cup butter or margarine
6 tbsps flour
1 bunch green onions, chopped
2oz parsley, chopped
2 tbsps Worcester sauce
½ tsp tabasco
Pinch salt
1 large or 2 small cooked crabs
4 slices bread, crusts trimmed and made into crumbs

Step 3 Turn the crabs over and push out the body with your thumbs.

1. Remove the oysters from their shells with a small, sharp knife. Place the oysters in a saucepan and strain over any oyster liquid. Add the fish stock and cook gently until the oysters curl around the edges. Remove the oysters, keep them warm and strain the liquid into a clean pan.

2. Add the cream to the oyster liquid and bring to the boil. Allow to boil rapidly for about 5 minutes.

3. Remove crab claws and legs. Turn the crabs over and push out the body with your thumbs.

4. Remove the stomach sac and lungs (dead man's fingers) and discard.

5. Cut the body in four sections with a large, sharp knife and pick out the meat with a skewer.

6. Crack claws and legs to extract the meat. Leave the small legs whole for garnish, if desired.

7. Scrape out the brown meat from inside the shell and combine it with the breadcrumbs and white meat from the body and claws.

8. Melt the butter or margarine in a medium-size saucepan and stir in the flour. Cook gently for 5 minutes. Add the onions and parsley and cook a further 5 minutes. Pour over the cream and fish stock mixture, stirring constantly. Add the Worcester sauce, tabasco and salt, and cook about 15-20 minutes over low heat, stirring occasionally. Fold in the crab meat and breadcrumb mixture.

9. Place the oysters in the bottom of a buttered casserole or in individual dishes and spoon the crab meat mixture on top. Broil to brown, if desired, and serve immediately.

Cook's Notes

Time
Preparation takes about 40 minutes and cooking takes about 30 minutes.

$ **Buying Guide**
If fresh oysters on the half shell and freshly cooked crabs are not available, substitute canned oysters and use their liquid for part of the fish stock measurement. Canned oysters will not need as long to cook. Canned or frozen crab meat may be used in place of the fresh crabs, substituting about 8oz for the fresh crab meat.

 Serving Ideas
If serving as a first course, this recipe will serve 6. Add French bread and a salad for a light main course.

SERVES 8

BACKBONE STEW

A mixture of three kinds of pepper is typically Cajun. Normally made with pork, this stew is also good with inexpensive cuts of lamb.

3lb middle neck or other neck cut of lamb
¼ tsp each cayenne, white and black pepper
Pinch salt
6 tbsps oil
2 onions, sliced
1 large red pepper, seeded and sliced
2 sticks celery, sliced
6 tbsps flour
2 cloves garlic, crushed
5 cups stock or water
2 tbsps chopped parsley

Step 1 Cut in between the bones to divide the meat into even-size pieces.

1. Cut the lamb between the bones into individual pieces. Sprinkle a mixture of red, white and black pepper and salt over the surface of the chops, patting it in well.

2. Heat the oil in a large stock pot or casserole and when hot add the meat, a few pieces at a time, and brown on both sides.

3. When all the meat is brown, remove to a plate and add the onions, pepper and celery to the oil. Lower the heat and cook to soften. Remove and set aside with the meat.

4. Add the flour to the remaining oil in the pan and stir well. Cook slowly until a dark golden brown. Add the garlic and stir in the stock or water. Return the meat and vegetables to the pan or casserole and bring to the boil. Cover and cook slowly for 1½-2 hours, or until the lamb is very tender. Sprinkle with parsley and serve immediately.

Step 1 Mix the peppers together and sprinkle over the surface of the meat, patting in well.

Step 2 Brown the meat, a few pieces at a time, over very high heat.

Cook's Notes

Time
Preparation takes about 25 minutes and cooking takes about 2 hours.

Variation
The stew may be prepared with pork chops, sliced pork loin or with an inexpensive cut of beef.

Preparation
The stew may be prepared in advance and kept in the refrigerator for up to 2 or 3 days. Reheat slowly. Flavors will intensify.

SERVES 4-6

Dirty Rice

The name comes from the mixture of finely chopped chicken livers,
celery, green pepper and onions that colours the rice.

1 cup long-grain rice
2 cups water
1lb chicken livers
1 stick celery, roughly chopped
1 green pepper, seeded and roughly chopped
2 medium onions, roughly chopped
2 tbsps oil
Salt and pepper
Chopped parsley to garnish

4. Heat the oil in a large frying pan and add the liver mixture. Cook over moderate heat, stirring gently.

5. Once the mixture has set, turn down the heat to very low, cover the pan and cook about 30-40 minutes, or until rich golden brown in color.

6. Stir in the cooked rice, fluffing up the mixture with a fork. Heat through, season to taste and serve garnished with chopped parsley.

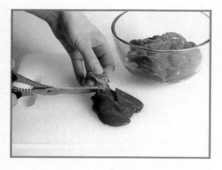

Step 2 Pick over chicken livers to remove fat and any discolored portions.

Step 4 Cook the liver mixture, stirring gently, in oil in a large frying pan.

Step 6 When the liver mixture has browned, stir in the cooked rice using a fork to fluff the mixture up.

1. Cook the rice in the water with a pinch of salt. When cooked, leave to stand while preparing the liver.

2. Pick over the chicken livers to remove any fat and discolored portions.

3. Place the livers, celery, pepper and onions in a food processor and process to finely chop the ingredients. The mixture will look soupy.

Cook's Notes

Time
Preparation takes about 20 minutes and cooking takes about 30-40 minutes.

Serving Ideas
The rice may be served as a main dish, in which case this recipe serves 2-3. The rice is often served cold as an appetizer. Also use the recipe as a side dish.

Cook's Tip
Removing the yellowish or greenish portions from the chicken liver will eliminate bitter taste.

SERVES 4

GINGERSNAP PORK CHOPS

Ginger-flavored cookies give a spicy lift to pork
chop gravy, thickening it at the same time.

4 even-sized pork chops, loin or shoulder
1 tsp ground black pepper
Pinch salt
1 tsp ground ginger
¼ tsp each rubbed sage, cayenne pepper, ground
 coriander and paprika
Pinch dried thyme
2 tbsps oil
2 tbsps butter
1 small onion, finely chopped
1 stick celery, finely chopped
½ clove garlic, crushed
1½ cups chicken stock
12-14 gingersnap cookies

Step 2 Brown the chops on both sides in the hot oil until golden.

1. Trim the chops if they have excess fat. Mix together the herbs and spices and press the mixture onto the chops firmly on both sides.

2. Heat the oil in a large frying pan and, when hot, add the chops. Brown on both sides and remove to a plate.

3. Add the butter to the frying pan and, when foaming, add the onions, celery and garlic. Cook to soften and pour on the stock.

4. Return the chops to the pan, cover and cook for about 30-40 minutes, or until tender.

5. When the chops are cooked, remove them to a serving dish and keep them warm. Crush the gingersnaps in a food processor. Alternatively, place the gingersnaps in a plastic bag and use a rolling pin to crush them. Stir the crushed gingersnaps into the pan liquid and bring to the boil.

6. Stir constantly to allow the gingersnaps to soften and thicken the liquid. Boil rapidly for about 3 minutes to reduce, and pour over the chops to serve.

Step 5 Use the crushed gingersnaps to thicken the pan liquid. Cook slowly until dissolved.

Cook's Notes

Time
Preparation takes about 20 minutes and cooking takes about 50 minutes.

Variation
Chicken or rabbit may be used in place of the pork.

Cook's Tip
The gingersnaps should thicken the cooking liquid sufficiently. If not, combine 2 tsps cornstarch with 1 tbsp water and some of the hot cooking liquid. Return to the pan and bring to the boil, stirring constantly until thickened and cleared.

SERVES 4

PIGEONS IN WINE

Pigeons are country fare and these are treated
in a provincial French manner with the Cajun touch
of white, black and red pepper.

4 pigeons
½ tsp each cayenne, white and black pepper
2 tbsps oil
2 tbsps butter or margarine
12oz button onions
2 sticks celery, sliced
4 carrots, peeled and sliced
4 tbsps flour
1½ cups chicken stock
½ cup dry red wine
4oz button mushrooms, quartered or left whole if small
3oz fresh or frozen lima beans
2 tsps tomato paste (optional)
2 tbsps chopped parsley
Pinch salt

Step 1 Season
the pigeons inside
their cavities with
the three kinds of
pepper.

1. Wipe the pigeons with a damp cloth and season them inside the cavities with the three kinds of pepper and a pinch of salt.

2. Heat the oil in a heavy-based casserole and add the butter or margarine. Once it is foaming, place in the pigeons, two at a time if necessary, and brown them on all sides, turning them frequently. Remove from the casserole and set them aside.

3. To peel the button onions quickly, trim the root ends slightly and drop the onions into rapidly boiling water. Allow it to come back to the boil for about 1 minute. Transfer to cold water and leave to cool completely. The skins should come off easily. Trim roots completely.

4. Add the onions, celery and carrots to the fat in the casserole and cook for about 5 minutes to brown slightly. Add the flour and cook until golden brown, stirring constantly.

5. Pour in the stock and the wine and stir well. Bring to the boil over high heat until thickened.

6. Stir in the tomato paste, if using, and return the pigeons to the casserole along with any liquid that has accumulated. Partially cover the casserole and simmer gently for about 40-45 minutes, or until the pigeons are tender. Add the mushrooms and lima beans halfway through the cooking time. To serve, skim any excess fat from the surface of the sauce and sprinkle over the chopped parsley.

Cook's Notes

Time
Preparation takes about 30 minutes and cooking takes about 50 minutes-1 hour.

Variation
The casserole may be prepared with Cornish hens quail or pheasant. The quail will take only half the cooking time.

Serving Ideas
This casserole is generally served from the dish in which it was cooked. Alternatively, arrange on individual plates, coat with some of the sauce and serve the rest separately. Accompany with rice.

SERVES 4-6

CHICKEN WITH EGGPLANT AND SMOKED HAM STUFFING

Eggplants and smoked ham are favorite Cajun ingredients.
They add interest to roast chicken in this rich stuffing.

3lb roasting chicken
1 small eggplant
2 tbsps butter or margarine
2 shallots, finely chopped
4oz smoked ham, chopped
1½ cups fresh breadcrumbs
1 tsp chopped fresh thyme
1 tsp chopped fresh oregano
2 tsps chopped parsley
Salt and pepper
Pinch cayenne pepper
1-2 eggs, beaten
2 tbsps additional butter, softened

Step 1 Sprinkle the cut surface of the eggplant lightly with salt and leave to stand.

1. Cut the eggplant in half lengthwise and remove stem. Lightly score the surface with a sharp knife and sprinkle with salt. Leave to stand for about 30 minutes for the salt to draw out any bitter juices.

2. Melt 2 tbsps butter in a medium saucepan and when foaming, add the shallots. Cook slowly to soften slightly.

3. Rinse the eggplant and pat dry. Cut into ½ inch cubes. Cook with the shallot until fairly soft. Add the remaining stuffing ingredients, beating in the egg gradually until the mixture just holds together. Add salt and pepper to taste.

4. Remove the fat from just inside the chicken cavity and fill with the stuffing. Tuck the wing tips under the chicken to hold the neck flap down. Stitch up the cavity opening on the chicken or secure with skewers. Tie the legs together and place the chicken in a roasting pan. Spread over the remaining softened butter and roast in a pre-heated 350°F oven for about 1 hour, or until the juices from the chicken run clear when the thickest part of the thigh is pierced with a sharp knife. Leave the chicken to stand for 10 minutes before carving. If desired, make a gravy with the pan juices.

Step 4 Before stuffing the chicken, remove the fat from just inside the cavity opening.

Cook's Notes

Time
Preparation takes about 30 minutes and cooking takes about 5-6 minutes for the stuffing and about 1 hour for the chicken.

Variation
Other ingredients, such as chopped red or green peppers, celery or green onions, may be added to the stuffing.

Watchpoint
Do not stuff the chicken until ready to cook.

SERVES 4

BRAISED RABBIT WITH PEPPERS

Rabbit was a staple in the diets of the early Cajun settlers,
who used local ingredients to vary this classic French game stew.

2¼lb rabbit joints
1 lemon slice
Flour for dredging
Pinch salt and pepper
1 tsp dry mustard
1 tsp paprika
¼ tsp each cayenne, white and black pepper
1 tsp garlic powder
¼ tsp dried dill
Oil for frying
1 onion, thinly sliced
1 small green pepper, seeded and thinly sliced
1 small red pepper, seeded and thinly sliced
14oz canned tomatoes
1 cup chicken stock
4 tbsps dry white wine
1 bay leaf

1. Soak the rabbit overnight with the lemon slice in cold water to cover.

2. Drain the rabbit and pat dry with paper towels.

3. Combine flour, spices, herbs and seasoning and dredge the rabbit with the mixture.

4. Heat the oil and fry the rabbit on all sides until golden brown. Remove to a plate.

5. Cook the onion and peppers for about 1 minute. Add the tomatoes, stock and bay leaf and bring to the boil. Return the rabbit to the pan and spoon over the sauce. Partially cover and cook over gentle heat until tender, about 45-50 minutes.

6. Add the wine during the last 10 minutes of cooking. Remove the bay leaf before serving.

Step 3 Dredge the rabbit in the seasoned flour mixture and shake off the excess.

Step 4 Heat the oil and fry the rabbit on both sides until golden brown.

Step 5 Cook the rabbit in the sauce with the peppers and onions until tender to the point of a knife.

Cook's Notes

Time
Preparation takes about 25 minutes, with overnight soaking for the rabbit. Cooking takes about 50 minutes-1 hour.

Variation
If yellow peppers are available, use the three colors for an attractive dish.

Cook's Tip
Soaking the rabbit with lemon overnight helps to whiten the meat and to remove any strong taste.

SERVES 4-6

CHICKEN AND SAUSAGE JAMBALAYA

A jambalaya varies according to what the cook has to hand.
It could contain seafood, ham, poultry, sausage or a tasty mixture.

3lbs chicken portions, skinned, boned, and cut into
  cubes
3 tbsps butter or margarine
1 large onion, roughly chopped
3 sticks celery, roughly chopped
1 large green pepper, seeded and roughly chopped
1 clove garlic, crushed
1 tsp each cayenne, white and black pepper
1 cup uncooked rice
14oz canned tomatoes
6 oz smoked sausage, cut into ½ inch dice
3 cups chicken stock
Salt
Chopped parsley

1. Use the chicken bones, skins, onion and celery trimmings to make stock. Cover the ingredients with water, bring to the boil and then simmer slowly for 1 hour. Strain and reserve.

2. Melt the butter or margarine in a large saucepan and add the onion. Cook slowly to brown and then add the celery, green pepper and garlic and cook briefly.

3. Add the three kinds of pepper and the rice, stirring to mix well.

4. Add the chicken, tomatoes, sausage and stock and mix well. Bring to the boil, then reduce the heat to simmering and cook about 20-25 minutes, stirring occasionally until the chicken is done and the rice is tender. The rice should have absorbed most of the liquid by the time it has cooked.

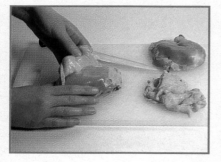

Remove the skin from the chicken and set aside.

Step 1 Put the skin and bones in a large stock pot with the onion and celery trimmings to make the stock. Add water to cover.

Cook's Notes

Time
Preparation takes about 35-40 minutes and cooking takes about 20-25 minutes.

Preparation
Check the level of liquid occasionally as the rice is cooking and add more water or stock as necessary. If there is a lot of liquid left and the rice is nearly cooked, uncover the pan and boil rapidly.

Serving Ideas
Jambalaya is often served as a first course, in which case this recipe serves 8. It can aslo be used as a side dish to serve 6 people.

SERVES 4-6

COUSH-COUSH (FRIED CORNMEAL)

Cornmeal is a favourite in the South, as a
bread, a coating for frying or a warming breakfast meal.

1½ cups yellow cornmeal
4 tbsps all-purpose flour
1 tbsp baking powder
2 tsps sugar
Pinch salt
2½ cups water
⅓ cup butter or margarine

Step 1 Combine the dry ingredients in a bowl and mix in the water gradually, stirring well to form a smooth paste.

1. Mix the cornmeal and the other dry ingredients in a large bowl and add the water gradually, mixing until smooth.

2. Melt the butter in a medium frying pan and, when foaming, add the cornmeal mixture, spreading it out smoothly in the pan.

3. Turn up the heat and fry until brown and crisp on the bottom.

4. Stir the mixture to distribute the brown crust.

5. Reduce the heat and cover the pan tightly.

6. Cook the mixture for about 10-15 minutes, stirring occasionally.

7. Spoon into serving bowls and serve hot.

Step 4 Stir the mixture to distribute the brown crust throughout it.

Cook's Notes

Time
Preparation takes about 15 minutes and cooking takes approximately 20-25 minutes.

Preparation
If necessary, add more water if the mixture seems too dry.

Serving Ideas
Serve for breakfast with fruit, jam, milk and sugar or syrups. Use a fruit syrup, maple syrup, cane sugar or golden syrup.

SERVES 6

SWEET POTATO PUDDING

The sweet potato reigns supreme in Southern cooking,
and this dish is satisfying either hot or cold.

1lb sweet potatoes
1 cup butter or margarine
¾ cup white sugar
¾ cup light brown sugar
4 eggs
2 cups all-purpose flour
1 tsp baking powder
½ tsp allspice
1 tsp ground nutmeg
½ tsp ground cinnamon
Pinch salt
½ cup milk

1. Peel the sweet potatoes, cut into cubes and place in boiling water to cover. Cook until tender, drain and leave to dry completely.

2. Cream the butter or margarine until light and fluffy and beat in the sugar gradually.

3. Beat in the eggs one at a time, beating well in between each addition.

4. Sift half the dry ingredients into the egg mixture and beat well. Add half the milk and then repeat with the remaining dry mixture and milk, beating well after each addition.

5. Mash the sweet potatoes and add to the flour and eggs. Lightly butter a baking dish and spread in the sweet potato mixture. Smooth the top and bake in a pre-heated 375°F oven for about 45 minutes, or until the top is firm to the touch. Allow to cool slightly before serving.

Step 3 Beat the eggs into the sugar and butter mixture one at a time.

Step 4 Gradually beat in the dry ingredients and the milk, alternating the two.

Step 5 Add the mashed sweet potato to the flour and egg mixture.

Cook's Notes

Time
Preparation takes about 20 minutes and cooking takes about 15-20 minutes for the sweet potatoes to cook and 45 minutes for the pudding to bake.

Variation
Add chopped nuts or raisins with the sweet potatoes.

Serving Ideas
Serve with pouring cream, lightly whipped cream or sour cream.

MAKES 12

Oreilles de Cochon

These light, delicate pastries have a rather
unusual name — Pig's Ears! It refers strictly
to the shape the dough takes when deep-fried.

1 cup all-purpose flour
1 tsp baking powder
¼ tsp salt
4 tbsps cold water
Oil for frying
1½ cups cane syrup mixed with ¾ cup molasses
3oz finely chopped pecans

Step 1 Sift the
dry ingredients
into a bowl and
make a well in the
center.

1. Sift the flour, baking powder and salt together in a large bowl. Make a well in the center and pour in the cold water.

2. Using a wooden spoon, mix until a stiff dough forms, and then knead by hand until smooth.

3. Divide the dough into 12 portions, each about the size of a walnut. Roll out each portion of dough on a floured surface until very thin.

4. Heat the oil in a deep fat fryer to 350°F. Drop each piece of pastry into the hot fat using two forks. Twist the pastry just as it hits the oil. Cook one at a time until light brown.

5. In a large saucepan, boil the syrup until it forms a soft ball when dropped into cold water.

6. Drain the pastries on paper towels after frying and dip carefully into the hot syrup. Sprinkle with pecans before the syrup sets and allow to cool before serving.

Step 3 On a
floured surface,
roll out each
piece until very
thin.

Cook's Notes

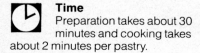

 Time
Preparation takes about 30
minutes and cooking takes
about 2 minutes per pastry.

Economy
When pecans are expensive,
substitute less expensive nuts
or omit entirely.

 Cook's Tip
The pastries must be served
on the day they are made
because they do not keep well.

MAKES 1 CAKE

SYRUP CAKE

Rather like gingerbread, but with a spicy taste of
cinnamon, nutmeg and cloves instead, this cake
can be served cool with coffee or tea or warm with cream.

1 cup vegetable shortening
1 cup molasses
3 eggs, beaten
3 cups all-purpose flour
1 tbsp baking powder
Pinch salt
1 tsp cinnamon
¼ tsp ground nutmeg
Pinch ground cloves
4 tbsps chopped pecans
4 tbsps raisins

3. Stir in the nuts and raisins and pour the mixture into a lightly greased 9 x 13″ baking pan.

4. Bake for about 45 minutes in a pre-heated 375°F oven.

5. To test for doneness, insert a skewer into the center of the cake. If it comes out clean, the cake is done. Allow to cool and cut into squares to serve.

Step 2 Sift in the dry ingredients and combine by hand.

Step 1 Cream the shortening until light and fluffy. Beat in the molasses with an electric mixer.

Step 5 Insert a skewer into the center of the cake. If it comes out clean the cake is done.

1. Cream the shortening until light and fluffy. Add the molasses and beat with an electric mixer. Add the eggs one at a time, beating well in between each addition.

2. Sift the flour together with a pinch of salt and baking powder. Combine with the molasses mixture and add the spices.

Cook's Notes

Time
Preparation takes about 20 minutes and cooking takes about 45 minutes.

Variation
The cake may be prepared without the nuts and raisins, if desired. Add vanilla extract or lemon rind, if desired, for extra flavor.

Cook's Tip
Lightly oil the inside of the measuring cup when measuring syrups like molasses. The syrup will not stick to the cup but will pour right out.

MAKES ABOUT 36

BROWN SUGAR COOKIES

This rather thick dough bakes to a crisp
golden brown cookie, perfect as an accompaniment
to ice cream or fruit salad.

1¼ cups packed light brown sugar
3 tbsps light corn syrup
4 tbsps water
1 egg
2⅓ cups all-purpose flour
1 tbsp ground ginger
1 tbsp bicarbonate of soda
Pinch salt
1 cup finely chopped pecans

Step 1 Combine the sugar, syrup, water and egg with an electric mixer until light.

1. Mix the brown sugar, syrup, water and egg together in a large bowl. Beat with an electric mixer until light.

2. Sift flour with the ginger, baking soda and salt into the brown sugar mixture and add the pecans. Stir by hand until thoroughly mixed.

3. Lightly oil three baking sheets and drop the mixture by spoonfuls about 2 inches apart.

4. Bake in a pre-heated 375°F oven until lightly browned around the edges, about 10-12 minutes. Leave on the baking sheet for 1-2 minutes before removing with a palette knife to a wire rack to cool completely.

Step 3 Use a spoon to drop the batter about 2 inches apart onto a greased baking sheet.

Step 4 Bake until browned around the edges. Cool slightly and remove with a palette knife.

Cook's Notes

Time
Preparation takes about 20 minutes and cooking takes about 10-12 minutes per batch.

Variation
Add raisins to the dough, or use other nuts instead of pecans.

Preparation
The dough will keep in the refrigerator for several days. Allow to stand at room temperature for at least 15 minutes before using.

MAKES 12-16

PRALINES

A sugary, crunchy and thoroughly delectable confection with pecans. These are a favorite treat in the Bayou country and all over the South.

1½ cups unsalted butter
1 cup sugar
1 cup packed light brown sugar
1 cup milk
½ cup heavy cream
1 cup chopped pecans
2 tbsps vanilla or rum extract
1 tbsp water
Butter or oil

Step 3 When pecans and liquid are added the mixture will foam. Stir until foam subsides.

Step 2 Simmer the sugar mixture until it is a deep golden brown.

Step 3 Drop the mixture by spoonfuls onto greased baking sheets.

1. Melt the butter in a large, heavy-based pan. Add the sugars, milk and cream and bring mixture to the boil, stirring constantly.

2. Reduce the heat to simmering and cook to a deep golden brown syrup. Stir continuously. After about 20 minutes, drop a small amount of the mixture into ice water. If it forms a hard ball, the syrup is ready. The hardball stage registers 250°F on a sugar thermometer.

3. Add the pecans, flavoring and water. Stir until the mixture stops foaming. Grease baking sheets with butter or oil and drop on the mixture by spoonfuls into mounds about 2 inches in diameter. The pralines will spread out as they cool. Allow to cool completely before serving.

Cook's Notes

 Time
Preparation takes about 25 minutes, and cooking takes about 20 minutes.

! **Watchpoint**
When adding the flavorings and water, the mixture may spatter and can burn the skin. Add liquid with a long-handled spoon or wear oven gloves.

 Variation
Pralines are popular when made with sesame seeds, too. Add them in place of pecans.

INDEX

Compiled by Judith Ferguson
Photographed by Peter Barry
Recipes Prepared for Photography by
Bridgeen Deery and Wendy Devenish